Roads and Trails

Terminology

NOVEMBER 2006

U.S. DEPARTMENT OF THE INTERIOR
BUREAU OF LAND MANAGEMENT
WASHINGTON D.C. 20240

Technical Note 422

Roads and Trails Terminology

A Joint Effort By

Division of Recreation and Visitor Services (WO-250)

and

Division of Engineering and Environmental Services (WO-360)

U.S. Department of the Interior

Bureau of Land Management

Recommended by:

[signature]   5/3/06

Division Chief, Division of Recreation and Visitor Services (WO-250)   Date

[signature]   5/3/06

Division Chief, Division of Engineering and Environmental
Services (WO-360)   Date

Approved by:

[signature]   5/12/06

Assistant Director, Renewable Resources and Planning (AD-200)   Date

[signature]   5-30-06

Assistant Director, Minerals, Realty and Resources Protection (AD-300)   Date

The Bureau of Land Management's (BLM) transportation system represents one of the most critical assets in the accomplishment of the BLM's mission to manage public lands. It affords entry for public access and provides the infrastructure that supports uses ranging from recreation to commercial activity and is the primary means of access to the 261.8 million acres under BLM jurisdiction.

Requirements associated with the effective stewardship of public lands, such as the Government Performance and Results Act, Federal Accounting Standards Advisory Board, Federal Land Policy and Management Act, and Off-Road Vehicle Executive Orders, continue to focus expectations internally and externally on a coordinated, consistent, and cohesive approach to the management of transportation-related linear features—generically referred to as routes—on public lands. The rationale for this effort is that the broad effect of the transportation system across the BLM's missions, strategic goals, and programs makes a consistent, organization-wide approach, rooted in common terms and definitions, an essential part of the management of public lands.

Several terms are used in reference to roads and trails on BLM lands. For purposes of this report, the term "linear features" has been used to describe transportation system-related "features," from engineered roadways with asphalt surfaces through challenging trails accessible only to nonmotorized traffic; "linear features" includes designated and nondesignated assets. The implementation of the Facility Asset Management System (FAMS) highlighted the need for a standard lexicon.

Abstract

Access to public lands is crucial for the effective use and stewardship of those lands. The Bureau of Land Management's (BLM) extensive transportation system provides the basis for access to the BLM's 261.8 million acres and supports all of the BLM's Strategic Goals as the "backbone" for administrative, commercial, and recreational use.

Because of the wide range of needs and uses, the BLM's routes represent a broad spectrum of linear features—from engineered roadways with asphalt surfaces through challenging trails accessible only to nonmotorized traffic. Inherent in the wide range of uses and "customers" is a varied vocabulary used to describe the linear features that includes roads, trails, paths, routes, and a host of derivatives of the basic terms. All of these terms have meaning and context within their respective programs but, when used collectively, often conflict and lead to confusion caused by the use of the same term to describe very different physical features.

The development of a consistent set of terms and definitions for use across the BLM is an essential first step to comprehensive travel management. By establishing a common set of terms and definitions, the foundation is established for effective interchange of management needs and information within and across programs. Standard terms and definitions also allow the BLM to communicate efficiently and consistently with customers and stakeholders.

The Roads and Trails Terminology Team was chartered to "*establish strategic direction and consistent terminology used by the recreation, planning, National Science and Technology Center (NSTC), National Landscape Conservation System (NLCS), lands, property, and engineering groups to manage the BLM transportation system in activities such as planning, inventorying, designating, mapping, signing, monitoring, developing public information, maintaining, assessing condition, tracking, and reporting data so ongoing alignment of current and future strategic comprehensive travel management and transportation objectives can be achieved.*" The present report represents the results of that effort and provides analysis, findings, and recommendations that address the key issues identified within the Team's charter (provided as Attachment 1).

The Roads and Trails Terminology Team (see Attachment 2 for a list of Team members), a joint effort between the National Recreation and Visitor Services Group, WO-250 (Recreation) and Protection and Response Group, WO-360 (Engineering) within the BLM, was formed to address critical issues surrounding the BLM approach to management of transportation linear features (such as routes, roads, trails, and paths). The issues included developing organization-wide approaches to:

1.   Establishing standard terms and definitions for the management of the BLM's linear assets that consistently identify, categorize, and track linear features that occur on the BLM's land, as well as those terms used to describe appropriate levels of stewardship to manage, protect, and preserve the public's assets.

2.   Developing processes for collection, storage, and management of data used to manage public lands and associated transportation system to include linear features identified for removal or reclamation, as well as those designated as part of the BLM's transportation system.

3.   Establishing a national data dictionary for all BLM roads, trails, and related items that provides the basis for consistency across the BLM in the management of data associated with linear features.

4.   Aligning the various programs responsible for travel management functions in a parallel fashion through the use of consistent terminology for conducting inventories, assessments, plans, monitoring, and other program functions.

The Team's approach to addressing these objectives included a combination of core team members and "advisors" (for a list of advisors, see Attachment 3) that represented the BLM's programs and allowed the Team to develop a comprehensive travel management approach suited to all the BLM's program needs. The Team, once engaged, realized a need to combine two of these objectives, as the data dictionary component relates to the collection, storage, and management of data. The result provided three objectives:

Objective 1. Establish Bureau Definitions and Standards for Transportation Linear Features

Objective 2. Determine Appropriate Minimum National Data Standards and Electronic Storage Location for Linear Feature Data (the integration of original objectives 2 and 3);

Objective 3. Develop a Strategy to Align the Inventory and Management of Transportation Linear Features between Resource Management Programs (formerly objective 4).

The process used to address the three objectives incorporated three steps:

- Understanding

- Analysis

- Findings and Recommendations

Through facilitated discussions within the core group and the advisors, each identified issue was reviewed to develop a clear *understanding* of the problem that included:

- Evaluation of the issue statement to define necessary outcomes and resolutions to achieve success

- Breadth of impact (programs affected, relations to non-BLM organizations, and legal or policy implications)

- Stakeholders

The Team's *analysis* of each issue included research into similar approaches taken by other Federal, State, and local agencies, as well as applicable private sector strategies, development of recommended approaches for consideration by the Team, and then vetting of those potential approaches within the Team and the advisor group to develop the Team's findings and recommendations for each established issue.

For clarity and a consistent understanding of the report's *findings and recommendations*, the following terms were established by the Roads and Trails Terminology Team:

- **Transportation Linear Features**—"Linear features" represents the broadest category of physical disturbance (planned and unplanned) on BLM land. Transportation-related linear features include engineered roads and trails, as well as user-defined, nonengineered roads and trails created as a result of the public use of BLM land.

Linear features may include roads and trails identified for closure or removal, as well as those that make up the BLM's defined transportation system.

- **Transportation System**—The "transportation system" represents the sum of the BLM's recognized inventory of linear features (roads, primitive roads, and trails) formally recognized, designated, and approved as part of the BLM's transportation system.

- **Routes**—"Routes" represents a group or set of roads, trails, and primitive roads that represents less than 100% of the BLM transportation system. Generically, components of the transportation system are described as routes.

- **Roads, Trails, and Primitive Roads**—These terms describe specific categories of transportation linear features and represent subsets of the BLM's transportation system.

- **Transportation Linear Disturbances**—"Linear disturbances" is used to identify human-made linear features that are not part of the BLM's transportation system. Linear disturbances may include engineered (planned) as well as unplanned single and two-track linear features that are not part of the BLM's transportation system.

The use of consistent terminology is at the heart of many of the issues identified by the Roads and Trails Terminology Team. The Proposed Comprehensive Travel Management Terminology Hierarchy (Figure 1) provides an organizational context for the linear features that exist on BLM land. Generally, those linear features are described in two categories: transportation system and transportation linear disturbances representing the human-made linear features that are not part of the transportation system.

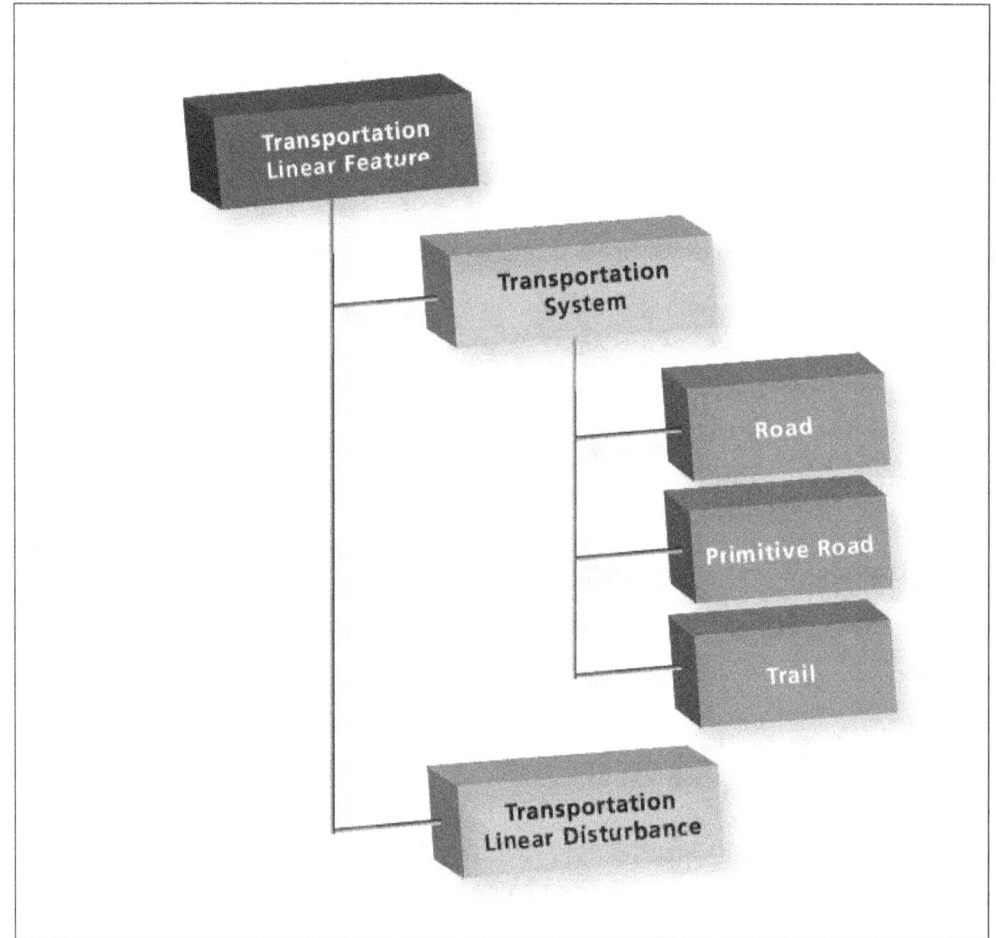

Figure 1. Proposed Comprehensive Travel Management Terminology Hierarchy.

Findings and recommendations were developed from the Team's research, analysis, and deliberation to address the identified issues. Findings were generally developed as a result of the Team's efforts to understand and "quantify" the issue, while the recommendations represent the culmination of the Team's research and analysis to develop suggested resolutions.

Detailed approaches in support of several of the recommendations were also developed by the Team for issues such as minimum national data standards and recommended definitions.

Additionally, some recommendations require development of an implementation plan, policy directives, or other related follow-up actions, including proposed "Action Plans" with preliminary schedules, responsibilities, and objectives.

Objective 1. Establish Bureau Definitions and Standards for Transportation Linear Features

Understanding

The Bureau of Land Management presently manages more than 82,000 miles of road and more than 16,000 miles of trail within the Facility Asset Management System (FAMS) that combine to traverse the BLM's 261.8 million acres of land. Many other miles of transportation-related linear features exist, yet are not actively managed.

A common lexicon and understanding of terms, definitions, and standards associated with the identification, description, and categorization of linear assets is essential to the effective communication and management of the BLM's assets. Common terms provide a wide range of benefits, including:

- Reasonable categorization and detail in the way the BLM identifies and describes its transportation assets.
- Consistent reporting to internal and external stakeholders and customers with respect to the size, type, quantity, designation, and use of the BLM's transportation assets.
- Auditable management strategies and asset inventories

Collectively consistent standards and definitions provide the basis for clear coordination and communication in the management of the BLM's transportation assets.

Analysis

Definitions and standards presently used to define and describe the BLM's transportation assets are contained within a myriad of documents, including BLM Recreation Manuals, Land-Use Planning Manuals, Engineering Manuals, Software System Manuals, Federal Regulations, and internal policy and guidance documents. Attachment 4 provides a list of the major documents reviewed by the Team.

Additionally, existing executive orders, laws, and statutory, regulatory, and policy guidance provide a framework within which many of the definitions and standards are required to function.

To clarify the problem, the Team conducted three, multiday workshops (in Phoenix, Sacramento, and Portland) in which the personnel present (core team and advisors) identified the types and characteristics of linear features that create the greatest challenges in consistency.

Pictures of existing BLM transportation linear features were used for the exercises that allowed each participant to identify and classify a common set of 20 photos (Attachment 12 contains the initial set of photos).

The results of the exercises indicated that the Team was relatively consistent in classifying engineered, low-clearance vehicle linear features as roads and single-track, linear features as trails, but was inconsistent in classifying two-track linear features.

Further analysis by the Team identified a common "disconnect" for those linear features that are not generally suited for low-clearance vehicular traffic, but which support 4 × 4 and high-clearance vehicle use. The following diagram (Figure 2) illustrates the type of transportation linear features (highlighted) that were identified as the source of confusion.

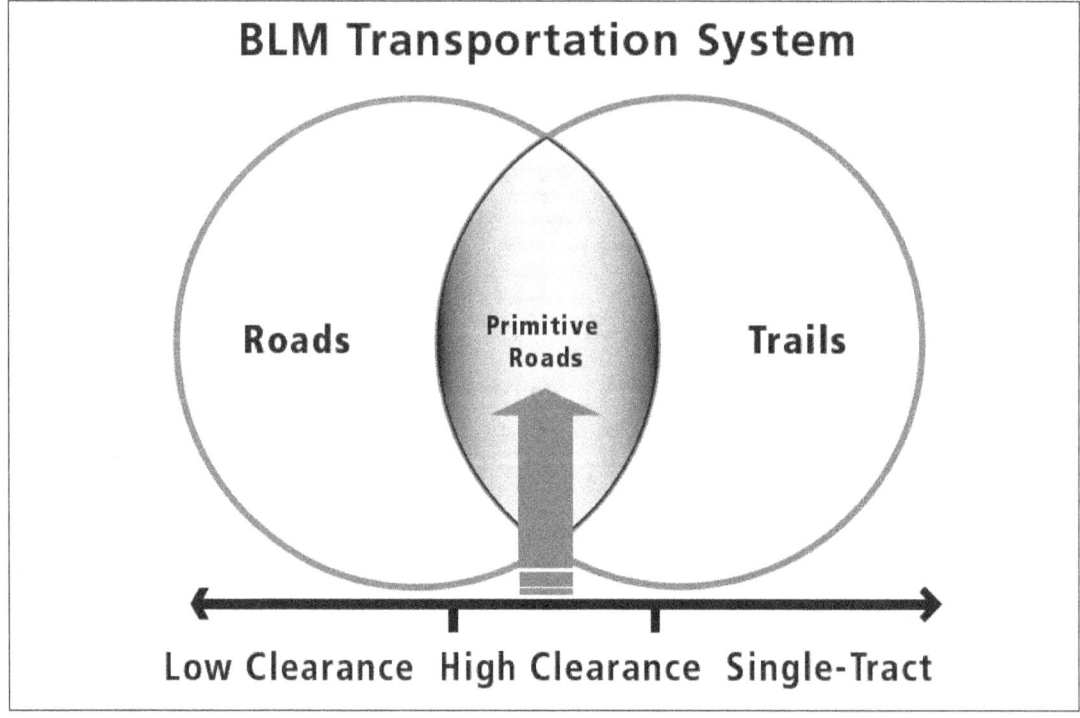

Figure 2. High-clearance, two-track linear features, such as primitive roads, were not consistently classified by the Roads and Trails Terminology Team.

Roads and trails are presently identified and defined in a number of BLM manuals and publications, yet none of those definitions seems to provide sufficient clarity to allow either the Team or BLM field personnel to classify transportation system linear assets consistently.

Research into common practices by other agencies, as well as State and local governments, identified "primitive roads" as a third category of routes presently used by a number of organizations to describe high-clearance and 4 × 4 routes that are not designed to an engineering standard, but are available for use and should be identified on transportation systems. Attachment 4 contains a list of documents that includes references to similar uses within State and local governments.

An exercise was undertaken by the Team with the representative photos of BLM routes to determine whether the introduction of a third asset category identified as "primitive roads" would provide sufficient delineation and address the needs of BLM programs. The results of that effort, as well as subsequent discussions with the Roads and Trails Terminology Team Advisors, indicated strong understanding and support for the introduction of the third asset classification.

The Team then developed a set of three basic definitions that describe a road, primitive road, and trail for use in categorizing BLM linear features that are part of the BLM's transportation system. Basic definitions for a road and primitive road were developed according to the BLM's 9100 Engineering Manual and the definition for a trail was developed from the Interagency Trail Data Standards.

The proposed standard terms and definitions were then reviewed against existing documents, known business rules, and identified requirements. On the basis of the review, potential issues and required actions were identified and addressed to ensure that the resulting definitions provide clear guidance and direction for the identification and classification of linear features that compose the BLM's transportation system.

Existing maintenance levels were also reviewed in conjunction with the development of the new asset categories for linear features. The Team's evaluation of the use of Maintenance Levels within the BLM also revealed inconsistent understanding and application of the present standards. In many instances, Maintenance Levels were poorly understood by field personnel and seemed to be mainly used to describe the type of linear feature (e.g., Maintenance Level 2 generally described a high-clearance or 4 × 4 accessible road) rather than the actual maintenance strategy or intensity determined by BLM management as being appropriate to the route.

To address this issue, the Team developed a recommendation to change Maintenance Levels to Maintenance Intensities and develop a consistent standard for use across all linear features.

Conclusions and Recommendations

1. *Standard Terms for Linear Features are based on three asset categories: "Road," "Primitive Road," and "Trail."*

Finding—The BLM's "transportation system" includes a broad range of linear assets well beyond those presently identified as "roads" and "trails" within the BLM inventory. BLM definitions presently used to identify and describe the BLM's linear assets vary within and across existing guidance documents. BLM definitions for defining, describing, and categorizing linear assets seem to provide insufficient guidance to existing personnel and allow for multiple interpretations that degrade the consistency of the BLM's inventory and reporting process. The Team concluded that reasonable, consistent, and auditable results are only achievable by institutionalizing a consistent set of terms and definitions across the BLM.

Recommendation—*Standardize the terms used as primary categories of transportation assets within the BLM as "Road," "Primitive Road," and "Trail."* Existing definitions for road and trail seem to provide inconsistent guidance for those linear assets that allow for motorized traffic of high-clearance vehicles but do not support low-clearance vehicles or use clear design standards. Descriptions and standards for describing and classifying these assets seem to allow the greatest level of inconsistency. Recommended definitions are:

- **Road:** A linear route declared a road by the owner, managed for use by low-clearance vehicles having four or more wheels, and maintained for regular and continuous use.
- **Primitive Road**: A linear route managed for use by four-wheel drive or high-clearance vehicles. Primitive roads do not normally meet any BLM road design standards.

- **Trail:** A linear route managed for human-powered, stock, or off-highway vehicle forms of transportation or for historical or heritage values. Trails are not generally managed for use by four-wheel drive or high-clearance vehicles.

The addition of a third major classification category (primitive roads) for linear assets is viewed by the Team as a key recommendation. Attachment 5 provides the Team's recommendations for an initial set of terms and definitions for use across all programs within the BLM when identifying, describing, or categorizing transportation assets.

2. *Change "Maintenance Levels" to "Maintenance Intensity" and simplify the standards for consistency across all linear features.*

Finding—Existing Maintenance Level definitions presently address both the type of road (road geometry or construction material) and the level of use but do not provide a clear standard for the actual maintenance level. As a result, they are used inconsistently across the BLM as a means for describing everything from road construction type through appropriate maintenance standards.

Recommendation—*Change "Maintenance Levels" to "Maintenance Intensity" and simplify the standards for consistency across all linear features.* The implementation of primary transportation asset categories provides an opportunity to review and enhance current standards for determining maintenance levels, managed use standards, and other descriptive information used to describe and report on the BLM's assets. Attachment 5 provides the Team's recommendations for the new Maintenance Intensity levels. It includes four primary Maintenance Intensity levels that allow for removal, low, medium, and high maintenance intensities, irrespective of the type of route (road, primitive road, or trail).

A draft Action Plan with recommended responsibilities and outcomes to support the transition of definitions and maintenance standards is provided as Attachment 6.

Objective 2. Determine Appropriate Minimum National Data Standards and Electronic Storage Location for Linear Feature Data

Understanding

Directions provided within Land-Use Plans are an important part of the BLM's strategic approach to stewardship of public lands. An integral component to the development, implementation, and management of the plans is an accurate knowledge of the transportation linear features identified on the BLM's 261.8 million acres. Information that describes the transportation linear features is presently collected through a myriad of efforts ranging from interpretation of aerial photography to field investigation utilizing remote sensing (Global Positioning System—GPS) equipment.

Data developed as a result of the management planning efforts are generally stored in a Geographical Information System (GIS). States and Field Offices presently use their own discretion in determining the appropriate information to collect and where the data will be stored after the planning effort.

Inconsistent standards across Field Offices and States have the potential to limit the functionality and long-term value of the data to the BLM, as well as affect the interoperability between programs (e.g., Recreation and Engineering).

Analysis

Existing references, including the *Interagency Trail Data Standards* and BLM Instruction Memorandum 2004-117, "Minimum National Data Standard for Roads," provide specific guidance on the format and content of linear feature data and were used as the baseline for the analysis.

The approach allowed the Team to focus on developing recommendations and business rules that align the location and storage of linear feature data in an approach consistent with the basic objectives and "customers" of the electronic systems (e.g., the Facility Asset Management System [FAMS] is the BLM's electronic system for asset management. Therefore, all asset management information should reside in FAMS).

The issue of determining which information should reside in the Facility Asset Management System (FAMS) versus the Recreation Management Information System (RMIS) or BLM-wide geographical information systems such as the National Integrated Land System (NILS) was reviewed to identify the customer for the information, which business functions the information supports, and key stakeholders for the information (see Attachment 11, Trail Data Standards Cross-Walk).

Linking the "customer" and "business purpose" to the potential information allowed the Team to develop a recommended approach for the storage of linear feature data and identify information that seemed to be beyond the "business purpose" of current national level electronic systems within the BLM.

Conclusions and Recommendations

3. *Develop and formalize through policy guidance the required minimum national data standard for all transportation linear features that compose the BLM transportation system.*

Finding—Present standards such as the "Interagency Trail Data Standards" and the Bureau of Land Management IM 2004-117, "Minimum National Data Standard for Roads," provide excellent sources for an organization-wide minimum national standard for roads, primitive roads, and trails. However, national-level guidance is not presently available for primitive roads and trails that indicates the appropriate minimum national data standards (a mandated and consistent set of linear feature data across the BLM), recommended data repository, or party responsible for maintaining all of the transportation linear feature data within the Bureau of Land Management.

Recommendation—*Develop and formalize through policy guidance the required minimum national data standard for all linear features that compose the BLM transportation system.* The required minimum national data standard should define the required minimum data standards that must be adhered to by all organizations within the BLM when planning, collecting, or managing linear feature data that is part of the BLM's transportation system. The minimum national data standard would not preclude the collection of additional information if deemed necessary, but would provide a consistent set of data across the entire BLM. Attachment 7 represents the Team's recommendation for a minimum national data standard for primitive roads and trails that incorporates data from the Interagency Trails Data Standard and existing Instruction Memorandum (IM 2004-117) on roads into two consistent requirements.

4. *Use the Facility Asset Management System (FAMS) as the system for the management of all Bureau of Land Management transportation system assets.*

Finding—BLM-wide information technology solutions such as the Facility Asset Management System (FAMS), Recreation Management Information System (RMIS), and National Integrated Land System (NILS) have each identified or "stated" business objectives that define their purpose and role within the Bureau of Land Management. Those business objectives or roles also define the appropriate location for the BLM's linear feature information and should serve as the guidance for the correct storage and management location for BLM linear feature information.

Recommendation—*Use the Facility Asset Management System (FAMS) as the system for the management of all Bureau of Land Management transportation system assets.* The term "assets" in this context represents linear features that have been formally identified (or "designated") as BLM assets versus the sum of all linear features on BLM land. Doing so allows the BLM to use a single set of data and provide consistent information internally and externally, as well as enhance efficiency through reduced duplication of effort and access to the same data across multiple programs.

5. *Develop a Minimum National Data Standard for the Collection of Transportation Linear Feature Data during Land-Use Planning and Related Efforts.*

Finding—Discussions with the programs engaged in land-use planning indicate a single, comprehensive BLM-wide approach to the collection and management of transportation linear feature information gathered as part of land-use planning efforts is not presently available. Moreover, such a national data standard would provide a consistent means of collecting a baseline data set for all linear features identified on BLM land.

Recommendation—*Develop a Minimum National Data Standard for transportation linear features that incorporates national data requirements from Recreation, NLCS, and Engineering and provides a consistent set of guidance to the Field.* Collection of information beyond the minimum national data standard is left to the discretion of the individual States and Field Offices. However, when data elements contained within the Interagency Trail Data Standards are used, collection of data should conform to the guidance provided in the most recent edition of the Interagency Trail Data Standards.

A draft "Action Plan" with recommended responsibilities and outcomes to support the implementation and standardization of minimum national data standards for all linear features included in the BLM asset inventory, as well as the broad-based use of the Facility Asset Management System across the BLM, is provided as Attachment 8.

Objective 3. Develop a Strategy to Align the Inventory and Management of Transportation Linear Features between Resource Management Programs

Understanding

Transportation linear features on BLM Lands compose one of the most significant issues facing the BLM and are the focus of a concentrated investment of BLM resources to adequately identify, categorize, designate, operate, and maintain. A comprehensive framework that identifies the relations, responsibilities, and interconnectivity between the various efforts is an essential element to the immediate and long-term objectives of the BLM's planning efforts.

Analysis

The Roads and Trails Terminology Team identified current efforts within the BLM that affect the management of linear features. Some of the programs that are directly engaged in those types of activities include:

- Recreation
- Engineering
- Minerals (Energy Development)
- Lands and Realty
- Wild Horse and Burro
- Budget and Performance
- National Science and Technology Center
- National Landscape Conservation System
- Fire
- Wildlife

Defining the roles of each organization and how management decisions are communicated, incorporated, maintained, and enforced is at the crux of an articulated comprehensive framework between the various activities.

The Team's findings with respect to the alignment between land-use planning and asset management highlight some of the specific issues and needs that surround the interrelations between land-use planning and the resource management of the BLM's transportation system.

Transportation linear features that exist on public lands are identified on a wide range of sources, from the BLM's internal databases through third-party publications, and the quantity, use, and location of those linear features may vary greatly depending on the sources. Such a range of sources complicates the effective communication of information and makes it difficult to accurately report on the BLM's inventory of roads, primitive roads, and trails.

Additionally, planning efforts associated with land and resource use represent a significant investment by the BLM in developing guidance and direction for the short- and long-term management of public lands. Given the level of investment and effort associated with completing the land-use plans, it is essential that the information and decisions they contain be preserved and implemented as part of the BLM's asset management program.

Finally, an integral part of asset management is an approach for modification, decommissioning, reclamation, or removal of transportation linear features that no longer meet the BLM's management objectives.

Conclusions and Recommendations

6. *Recognize the Facility Asset Management System (FAMS) inventory of routes as the BLM's current transportation system.*

Finding—The BLM does not have a BLM-wide standard for what constitutes the current recognized transportation system. While various programs within the BLM provide data and maps that depict the BLM's transportation system, no single organization or data system is identified as the "standard" within the BLM. As a result, projections and reports of the total miles within the BLM's transportation system vary significantly depending on the source of information and cause the BLM challenges in addressing annual financial audit, Government Performance and Results Act, and other reporting requirements.

Recommendation—Recognize the Facility Asset Management System (FAMS) as the initial inventory of the BLM's transportation system. FAMS presently contains 82,000 miles of road and 16,000 miles of trails that are used to report the BLM's asset inventory and deferred maintenance requirements and develop annual maintenance needs. FAMS represents the "baseline" for the BLM's current transportation system and comprises the designated roads and trails within the BLM. Formal recognition of FAMS as the baseline will provide consistency between all BLM Programs.

7. *Implement a BLM-wide policy that requires any change in the BLM's inventory of designated roads, primitive roads, and trails to occur through the land-use planning process.*

Finding—A BLM-wide policy that provides management controls on changes to the designated inventory of routes within the BLM's transportation system operates informally but does not exist as part of formal guidance or policy.

Recommendation—*Implement a BLM-wide policy that requires any change in the BLM's designated transportation system to occur through the land-use planning process.* Changes to the BLM's designated transportation system should occur as part of the formal evaluation and designation process through one of four events:

- Record of Decision (ROD) for a Resource Management Plan/Environmental Impact Statement (RMP/EIS) or an Amendment or Revision of an RMP/EIS.
- Decision Record for an Activity Plan, Plan Amendment/Environmental Assessment (EA).
- Federal Register Notice Action (under the authority of 43 CFR 8341.2, 8364.1, 8365.1-6, or 9268.3) that has a follow-up land-use planning action and associated NEPA action.
- Management decision of appropriate routes in an area that has been designated open to off-highway vehicle use.

The recommended approach for implementation of guidance between the land-use planning and formalized recognition and management of routes within FAMS is an Instruction Memorandum (IM) that clearly identifies the appropriate process for formal changes to the BLM's transportation system asset inventory.

8. *Develop a comprehensive travel management policy for land-use planning guidance to facilitate a consistent approach and process across the BLM.*

Finding—BLM guidance for transportation-related land-use planning is presently contained in a wide range of documents, from BLM manuals through planning handbooks. The lack of a single, comprehensive source of guidance contributes to the difficulty in providing consistency in the process and its application within the BLM.

Recommendation—*Develop comprehensive travel management policy guidance on land-use planning to facilitate a consistent approach and process across the BLM.* Travel planning and management guidance presently exists in a number of locations. Develop a BLM comprehensive travel management source guide for use across the BLM that provides consistency within the BLM and also minimizes the effort required to maintain BLM guidance.

Attachment 9 provides a draft "Action Plan" with recommended responsibilities and outcomes to support the standardization of comprehensive travel management planning guidance in a source guide.

9. *The BLM should develop policy guidance to identify, track, monitor, prioritize, and fund the removal of unwanted transportation linear features (routes and other linear disturbances on BLM land).*

Finding—A BLM-wide approach to addressing transportation linear features identified as part of the land-use planning process, but not designated as part of the BLM's transportation system, does not exist. States and Field Offices presently address the issue with approaches that range from abandonment through aggressive remediation. Lack of a nationwide approach to address the need makes it extremely difficult for the BLM to even articulate the full extent of the requirement, let alone proactively resolve it.

Recommendation—*The BLM should develop policy guidance and implement a formalized approach to identify, track, monitor, prioritize, and fund the removal of transportation linear features (routes and other linear disturbances on BLM land).* A formalized approach to the mitigation of existing transportation linear features through decommissioning, reclamation, or modification of use is an integral part of the implementation of land-use planning efforts. Formalizing the BLM's approach to addressing these needs provides a consistent advocacy for seeking funding through internal and external funding sources, developing priorities, and monitoring the progress of the BLM's efforts to implement the land-use plans. A draft "Action Plan" with recommended responsibilities and outcomes to support the development of a BLM-wide approach to address unwanted linear features is provided as Attachment 10.

Attachment 1. Roads and Trails Terminology Team Charter

Purpose

The purpose of the Roads and Trails Terminology Team is to establish strategic direction and consistent terminology used by the recreation, planning, National Science and Technology Center (NSTC), National Landscape Conservation System (NLCS), lands, property, and engineering groups to manage the BLM transportation system in activities such as planning, inventorying, designating, mapping, signing, monitoring, developing public information, maintaining, assessing condition, tracking, and reporting data so ongoing alignment of present and future strategic comprehensive travel management and transportation objectives can be achieved.

Objectives

Specific objectives of this team effort are to:

1)   Establish BLM definitions for the many different types of roads, trails, and other associated terms (e.g., maintenance levels) that are used when managing these assets.

2)   Determine what information on roads and trails will be stored in the Facility Asset Management System (FAMS), as well as in other existing data management systems.

3)   Establish a national travel management data dictionary for all roads, trails, and closely associated linear feature travel and transportation management terminology.

4)   Develop a strategy that aligns the various programs responsible for travel management functions in a parallel fashion through the use of consistent terminology for conducting inventories, assessments, plans, monitoring, and other program functions.

Membership

The National Recreation Group representative (WO-250) and National Engineering Group representative (WO-360) will co-chair the Team. The Team will consist of a facilitator, note taker, and representatives from recreation, planning, NSTC, NLCS, lands, property, and engineering groups as core members and advisors. In addition, representatives from the field and State level, Recreation Visitor Services Advisory Team, the Engineering Advisory Team, as well as others will be included as appropriate. The temporary services of a contractor will be employed to assist with meeting note-taking, writing and editing draft reports, finalizing reports, printing, and distributing final Team products.

Schedule

The Team will convene for three, 1-week sessions in September, October, and November of 2004.

Deliverables

The final report will be submitted to the Assistant Director, Renewable Resources & Planning (AD-200), and Assistant Director, Minerals, Realty & Resources Protection (AD-300), by January 30, 2005, and will include:

- An updated list of terminology and definitions along with an interpretation for various applications.
- A coordination and integration strategy between FAMS, GIS, and RMIS for roads and trails planning and management.
- A travel management data dictionary for all roads, trails, and associated linear travel and transportation structures.
- A strategy to coordinate and merge the roads and trails inventory effort with condition assessments of those assets.
- A strategy to merge the inventory of roads and trails with land-use plan and recreation databases for the identification, designation, and management of travel management networks.

(signature)   9/9/04

(Approved) Group Manager (WO-250)   **Date**

(signature)   9-9-04

(Approved) Group Manager (WO-360)   **Date**

Attachment 2. Roads and Trails Terminology Core Team Members

Name	Organization	Phone
Mark Goldbach	WO-250 (Co-Chair)	202-452-5176
Elliot Ng	WO-360 (Co-Chair)	202-557-3564
Gery Behr	WO-850 (Facilitator)	303-236-0478
Terry Heslin	ID- 931	208-378-3836
Bill Gibson	AZ-931	602-417-9425
Stuart Cox	CO-952	303-239-3805
Dick Bergen	OR-959	503-808-6100
Casey Matthews	UT-952	801-539-4199
Eric Dillinger	Carter & Burgess, Inc.	817-735-6794
Ellen Crews	Carter & Burgess, Inc.	817-735-6044
Shelley Wolff	HNTB Companies	816-527-2482

Attachment 3. Team Advisors and Guests

Advisor Name	Organization
Deb Salt	WO-172 NLCS
Paul Graves	ST-122 National Science and Technology Center
John Bell	USDA Forest Service Washington Office (Road System Operation & Maintenance Engineer)
Steve Anderson	CA-360 Redding Field Office
Dick Todd	WO-350 Lands and Realty
Chris Hamilton	WO-330 LRPO
Tina McDonald	WO-250 Recreation Division
Neffra Matthews	ST-122 National Science and Technology Center
Jim Perry	WO-310 Fluid Minerals
Gary Pavick	WO-172 Wilderness/NLCS
Scott Florence	WO-210 Planning
Phil Daemon Damon	ID-320 Pocatello Field Office
Paul Fredericks	OR-959 Oregon State Office
Guest Name	Organization
Paul Fulkerson	CA-944 California State Office
Miles Brown	OR-933 Oregon State Office
Ron Price	OR-930 Oregon State Office
Thomas W. Erkert	USDA FS Regional 6 Office (Group Leader, Transportation Planning Operation & Maintenance)
Richard Hanes	OR-933 Oregon State Office

Attachment 4. List of Documents Reviewed

1. Travel Routes. National Data Dictionary, ROADS, Infrastructure Application, Version 1.3, January 2003.

2. Off-Highway Vehicle (OHV) Designations.

3. UTAH BLM GIS Data Standards, January 22, 2004.

4. UT 2004-061, Designating Off Highway Vehicle Routes in the Land Use Planning Process, 2004.

5. US Forest Service, Glossary of Road Terms, 2004.

6. Presentation, National Integrated Land System (NILS), 2004.

7. IM-No. 1999-211, Subject—Facilities Maintenance, 9/29/99.

8. Memo from EAT roads committee to Director WO-300, Subject: Transportation and Deferred Management Maintenance, 8/20/1999.

9. Memo from EAT roads committee to Director, WO-300, Subject: BLM Roads and Trails System Management, 8/31/1999.

10. BLM Roads Presentation to the DOI Conference, 2004.

11. BLM Comprehensive Travel Management Presentation, 2004.

12. Alamosa Colorado, Visitor Information Center Brochure, 2004.

13. Arizona State Statute, 28-6705, "Primitive Roads Designation."

14. U.S. Forest Service, Sumter National Forest Camping Guide, Southern Region, 2004.

15. Great Sand Dunes National Preserve, National Park Service Literature, 2004.

16. Grand Canyon National Park, Wilderness Management Plan, National Park Service, 2003.

17. Washington State Statute, RCW 36.75.300, "Primitive roads—Classification and Designation."

18. Pima County Arizona, Primitive Road Definition and Statute, 2004.

19. Bureau of Reclamation, Prineville Reservoir Resource Management Plan, 2003.

20. IB-2000-005, Subject: Road and Trail Condition Assessment, 10/20/1999.

21. IB-2000-092, Subject Transportation Management Re-Engineering, 3/23/2000.

22. Draft Report of Transportation System Management Re-Engineering, 10/2001

23. FIMMS FY2002 Roads data, 11/5/2002.

24. Draft Memorandum: Lynn Scarlett, Assistant Secretary-Policy Management and Budget, Subject: Standard Facilities Data Requirements, 2002.

25. Federal Accounting Standards Advisory Board. 1996. Accounting for Property, Plant, and Equipment. Statement of Recommended Accounting Standards, Number 6. Amended.

26. Governmental Performance and Results Act.

27. Bureau of Land Management Strategic Plan.

28. Bureau of Land Management, Roads Team Meeting Report #1, June 2002.

29. Bureau of Land Management, Roads Team Meeting Report #2, July 2003.

30. Instruction Memorandum 2004-117, Minimum National Data Standard for BLM Roads.

31. Federal Highway Administration and U.S. Fish and Wildlife Service, Guidance on the Federal Highways Refuge Roads Program, 2000.

32. King County Roads Standards, King County, Washington, 2002.

33. A Guide for Local Area Road Managers, Washington Department of Transportation, 1994.

34. Evaluation of Expenditures on Rural Roads in Kansas, Kansas University Transportation Center, 2002.

35. Review of Funding Needs for Pavement Preservation, City of Eugene, Oregon, 2001.

36. Department of Interior, National Park Service, Federal Lands Highway Program FY 2004 Overview and Budget Justifications, 2003.

37. Federal Lands Highway Program—Park Roads and Parkways Program: Service-wide Transportation Planning, Design, and Construction Program, February 27, 2003.

38. Federal Lands Highway Program Park Roads and Parkways Revised Funding and Prioritization Procedures, Federal Lands Highway Program, 1998.

39. Asset Management Primer, U.S. Department of Transportation, 1999.

40. AASHTO Pavement Management Catalogue, AASHTO, 2002.

41. Executive Order 11644, Use of Off-Road-Vehicles on the Public Lands, 1972.

42. Executive Order 11989, Off-Road-Vehicles on the Public Lands, 1977.

43. National Management Strategy for Motorized Off-Highway Vehicle on Public Lands, Department of Interior, Bureau of Land Management, 2001.

44. National Mountain Bicycling Strategic Action Plan, Department of Interior, Bureau of Land Management, November 2002.

45. Instruction Memorandum No. UT 2004-040, GIS Data Standard for Off Highway Vehicle Area Designations, February 2004.

46. Interagency Trail Data Standards, Version 1.1, April 28, 2004.

Attachment 5. Terms, Definitions, and Maintenance Intensity Standards

DEFINITIONS:

TRANSPORTATION SYSTEM LINEAR FEATURES (ASSETS):

Road: A linear route declared a road by the owner, managed for use by low-clearance vehicles having four or more wheels, and maintained for regular and continuous use.

Primitive Road: A linear route managed for use by four-wheel drive or high-clearance vehicles. These routes do not normally meet any BLM road design standards.

Trail: A linear route managed for human-powered, stock, or off-highway vehicle forms of transportation or for historical or heritage values. Trails are not generally managed for use by four-wheel drive or high-clearance vehicles.

OTHER TERMS USED IN THIS REPORT:

Assets—Term used to describe roads, primitive roads, and trails that comprise the transportation system. Also the general term used to describe all BLM-constructed "Assets" contained within the Facility Asset Management System (FAMS).

Closed Area—An area where off-highway vehicle use is prohibited. Use of off-highway vehicles in closed areas may be allowed for certain reasons; however, such use shall be made only with the approval of the authorized officer.

Comprehensive Travel Management—The proactive interdisciplinary planning, on-the-ground management, and administration of travel networks (both motorized and nonmotorized) to ensure that public access, natural resources, and regulatory needs are considered. It consists of inventory, planning, designation, implementation, education, enforcement, monitoring, easement acquisition, mapping and signing, and other measures necessary for providing access to public lands for a wide variety of uses (including uses for recreational, traditional, casual, agricultural, commercial, educational, and other purposes).

Designated Roads and Trails—Specific roads and trails identified by the BLM (or other agencies) where some type of motorized vehicle use is appropriate and allowed either seasonally or yearlong. (BLM Manual H-1601-1, Land Use Planning Handbook)

Limited Area—An area restricted at certain times, in certain areas, or to certain vehicular use. These restrictions may be of any type but can generally be accommodated within the following categories: Numbers of vehicles; types of vehicles; time or season of vehicle use; permitted or licensed use only; use on existing roads and trails; use on designated roads and trails; and other restrictions.

Maintenance Intensities–Transportation System Assets—BLM Route Maintenance Intensities provide guidance for appropriate "standards of care" to recognized routes within the BLM. Recognized Routes by definition include Roads, Primitive Roads, and Trails carried as Assets within the Bureau of Land Management Facility Asset Management System (FAMS).

Maintenance Intensities provide consistent objectives and standards for the care and maintenance of BLM routes according to identified management objectives. Maintenance Intensities are consistent with land-use planning management objectives (for example, natural, cultural, recreation setting, and visual). Maintenance Intensities provide operational guidance to field personnel on the appropriate intensity, frequency, and type of maintenance activities that should be undertaken to keep the route in acceptable condition and provide guidance for the minimum standards of care for the annual maintenance of a route.

Maintenance Intensities do not describe route geometry, types of route, types of use, or other physical or managerial characteristics of the route. Those items are addressed as other descriptive attributes to a route.

Maintenance Intensities provide a range of objectives and standards, from "identification for removal" through frequent and intensive maintenance.

Level 0   **Maintenance Description:** Existing routes that will no longer be maintained or declared as routes. Routes identified as Level 0 are identified for removal from the Transportation System entirely.

Maintenance Objectives:
- No planned annual maintenance
- Meet identified environmental needs
- No preventive maintenance or planned annual maintenance activities

Maintenance Funds: No annual maintenance funds

Level 1 **Maintenance Description:** Routes where minimal (low-intensity) maintenance is required to protect adjacent lands and resource values. These roads may be impassable for extended periods of time.

Maintenance Objectives:

- Low (Minimal) maintenance intensity
- Emphasis is given to maintaining drainage and runoff patterns as needed to protect adjacent lands. Grading, brushing, or slide removal is not performed unless route bed drainage is being adversely affected, causing erosion.
- Meet identified resource management objectives
- Perform maintenance as necessary to protect adjacent lands and resource values
- No preventive maintenance
- Planned maintenance activities limited to environmental and resource protection
- Route surface and other physical features are not maintained for regular traffic

Maintenance Funds: Maintenance funds provided to address environmental and resource protection requirements. No maintenance funds provided to perform preventive maintenance.

Level 2 *RESERVED FOR POSSIBLE FUTURE USE*

Level 3 **Maintenance Description:** Routes requiring moderate maintenance because of low-volume use (e.g., seasonally or year-round for commercial, recreational, or administrative access). Maintenance Intensities may not provide year-round access, but are intended to generally provide resources appropriate for keeping the route in use for the majority of the year.

Maintenance Objectives:

- Medium (Moderate) maintenance intensity
- Drainage structures will be maintained as needed. Surface maintenance

will be conducted to provide a reasonable level of riding comfort at prudent speeds for the route conditions and intended use. Brushing is conducted as needed to improve sight distance when appropriate for management uses. Landslides adversely affecting drainage receive high priority for removal; otherwise, they will be removed on a scheduled basis.

- Meet identified environmental needs
- Generally maintained for year-round traffic
- Perform annual maintenance necessary to protect adjacent lands and resource values
- Perform preventive maintenance as required to generally keep the route in acceptable condition
- Planned maintenance activities should include environmental and resource protection efforts, annual route surface
- Route surface and other physical features are maintained for regular traffic

Maintenance Funds: Maintenance funds provided to preserve the route in the present condition, perform planned preventive maintenance activities on a scheduled basis, and address environmental and resource protection requirements.

Level 4   *RESERVED FOR POSSIBLE FUTURE USE*

Level 5   **Maintenance Description:** Routes for high (Maximum) maintenance because of year-round needs, high-volume traffic, or significant use. Also may include routes identified through management objectives as requiring high intensities of maintenance or to be maintained open year-round.

Maintenance Objectives:
- High (Maximum) maintenance intensity
- The entire route will be maintained at least annually. Problems will be repaired as discovered. These routes may be closed or have limited access because of weather conditions but are generally intended for year-round use.
- Meet identified environmental needs
- Generally maintained for year-round traffic

- Perform annual maintenance necessary to protect adjacent lands and resource values
- Perform preventive maintenance as required to generally keep the route in acceptable condition
- Planned maintenance activities should include environmental and resource protection efforts, annual route surface
- Route surface and other physical features are maintained for regular traffic

Maintenance Funds: Maintenance funds provided to preserve the route in the present condition, perform planned preventive maintenance activities on a scheduled basis, and address environmental and resource protection requirements.

Off-Highway Vehicle (off-road vehicle)—Any motorized vehicle capable of—or designated for—travel on or immediately over land, water, or other natural terrain, excluding: (1) any nonamphibious registered motorboat; (2) any military, fire, emergency, or law enforcement vehicle while being used for emergency purposes; (3) any vehicle whose use is expressly authorized by the authorized officer, or otherwise officially approved; (4) vehicles in official use; and (5) any combat or combat support vehicle when used for national defense.

Open Area—An area where all types of vehicle use is permitted at all times, anywhere in the area subject to the operating regulations and vehicle standards set forth in 43 CFR 8341 and 8342.

Transportation Linear Disturbances—Human-made linear features that are not part of the BLM's Transportation System. Linear disturbances may include engineered (planned), as well as unplanned single- and two-track linear features.

Transportation Linear Features—The broadest category of physical disturbance (planned and unplanned) on BLM land. Transportation-related linear features include engineered roads and trails, as well as user-defined, nonengineered roads and trails created as a result of the public use of BLM land. May include roads and trails identified for closure or removal, as well as those that make up the BLM's defined transportation system.

Transportation Plan—A transportation facility plan shown on forms and maps of all existing and planned access routes needed to use, protect, and administer the public lands. (Preparation of the transportation plan does not depend on RMPs; but as they are completed, the transportation plan should be revised to reflect changes.) (BLM Manual 9100—Engineering)

Transportation System—The sum of the BLM's recognized inventory of linear features (roads, primitive roads, and trails) formally recognized and approved as part of the BLM's transportation system.

Travel Management Areas—Polygons or delineated areas where a rational approach has been taken to classify areas as open, closed, or limited; and where a network of roads, trails, ways, and other routes that provide for public access and travel across the planning area are identified or designated. All designated travel routes within travel management areas should have a clearly identified need and purpose, as well as clearly defined activity types, modes of travel, and seasons or time frames for allowable access or other limitations (BLM Manual H-1601-1, Land Use Planning Handbook).

Way—Roadlike feature used by vehicles having four or more wheels but not declared a road by the owner and which receives no maintenance to guarantee regular and continuous use.

Attachment 6. Action Plan—Terms, Definitions, and Maintenance Intensities
Bureau of Land Management

ACTION PLAN	
Subject:	Update Terms, Definitions, and Maintenance Levels
Lead:	WO-360
Due Date:	
Reviewer:	
OBJECTIVE 1, RECOMMENDATION 1	

1. **Objective:**
    The Objective of this Action Plan is to update the Bureau of Land Management's existing guidance documents (manuals, handbooks, and related publications) so that they incorporate the new terms, definitions, and Maintenance Level (Maintenance Intensity) guidance developed by the BLM Roads and Trails Terminology Team.

2. **Action Plan Tasks:**
    ♦ Initiate after Approval of the Roads and Trails Terminology Report
    ♦ Assemble team to identify existing guidance documents for revision:
      • BLM 9100 Series Engineering Manuals
      • BLM "Gold Book"
      • BLM land-use planning process and documents
      • Facility Asset Management System (FAMS) data standards
      • Facility Asset Management System (FAMS) Maintenance Level designations
      • Minimum National Data Standard—BLM Roads
      • Condition Assessment Protocols—Roads, Primitive Roads, and Trails
      • BLM Real Property and "Asset" Standards
    ♦ Update existing documents in accordance with Roads and Trails Terminology Report
    ♦ Update existing documents published by BLM and provided to customers to reflect new designations

3. **Responsible Organization(s):**
    WO-250 and WO-360 are each to assign an individual as "lead" to identify and update appropriate guidance. WO-360 is responsible for Engineering and Asset Management-related information; WO-250 is to update land-use planning documents.

4. **Outcomes:**
    Consistent terms, definitions, and maintenance needs within the BLM, as well as an "alignment" of existing terms and definitions across multiple programs within the BLM.

Attachment 7. Proposed Minimum National Data Standards

This attachment contains three tables outlining assets, data elements, and status for:

- Approved National Data Standard for Roads

- Proposed National Data Standard for Primitive Roads

- Proposed National Data Standard for Trails

Approved National Data Standard for Roads

Asset	Data Element	Status
Road	Latitude	Required
	Longitude	Required
	Meridian	Required
	Township	Required
	Range	Required
	Section	Required
	Aliquot Part	Required
	Functional Class	Required
	Seismic Zone	Optional
	Congressional District	Required
	Locator Code	Required
	Easements Needed	Required
	Admin State	Required
	Geographic State	Required
	OR–CA Land	Required
	Route Number	Required
	Spur Number	Required
	Begin Route	Required
	Terminus	Required
	Year Withdrawn	Required
	Road Restrictions	Optional
	County	New in Phase II
	Jurisdiction	New in Phase II
	Master AUC	New in Phase II
Segment	Begin Mile	Required
	End Mile	Required
	Use Period Begin (Gone)	Optional
	Use Period End (Gone)	Optional
	Open in Jan	Optional
	Open in Feb	Optional
	Open in Mar	Optional
	Open in Apr	Optional
	Open in May	Optional
	Open in Jun	Optional
	Open in Jul	Optional
	Open in Aug	Optional
	Open in Sep	Optional
	Open in Oct	Optional
	Open in Nov	Optional

Approved National Data Standard for Roads

Asset	Data Element	Status
	Open in Dec	Optional
	County	Required
	Jurisdiction	Required
	Maintenance Responsibility	Required
	Maintenance Level	Required
	Condition (On Main Screen)	Required
	Surface Type	Required
	Average Width	Required
	Restrictions	Optional
	Asset Category Code (On Main Screen)	Required
	Year Constructed (On Main Screen)	Optional
	Design Speed	Optional
	OR–CA Land	Required
	Year Withdrawn	Optional
	Road Restrictions	Optional
	Road Surface	Required
	Congressional District	Required
	Meridian	Required
	Township	Required
	Range	Required
	Section	Required
	Aliquot Part	Required
	Special Designation—Ground Transportation Network (GTRN)	New in Phase II
	Road Closure Reason Code—GTRN	New in Phase II
	Road Closure Status Code—GTRN	New in Phase II
	No. of Lanes	New in Phase II
	Access Rights—GTRN	New in Phase II
	AUC—GTRN	New in Phase II
	TMO—Action Reason—GTRN	New in Phase II
	TMO—Action—GTRN	New in Phase II
	Route No.—GTRN	New in Phase II
	TMO—Approved by—GTRN	New in Phase II
	TMO—Benefit—GTRN	New in Phase II
	TMO—Planned Year—GTRN	New in Phase II
	TMO—Action Reason—GTRN	New in Phase II
	TMO—Action—GTRN	New in Phase II
Drain Dip	Mile Post	Optional
	Square Feet	Optional
	Depth	Optional

Approved National Data Standard for Roads

Asset	Data Element	Status
	Drainage Dip (Deleted)	Optional
Water Bar	Mile Post	Optional
	Square Feet	Optional
	Height	Optional
	Water Bar (Deleted)	Optional
Leadoff Ditch	Mile Post	Optional
	Location	Optional
	Leadoff Ditch (Deleted)	Optional
	Length	Optional
Low Water Crossing	Mile Post	Optional
	Square Feet	Optional
	Low Water Crossing Material	Optional
	Low Water Crossing (Deleted)	Optional
Ford	Mile Post	Optional
	Ford (Deleted)	Optional
Check Dam	Mile Post	Optional
	Check Dam (Deleted)	Optional
	Location	Optional
Rock Spillway	Mile Post	Optional
	Rock Spillway	Optional
Cross Drain Culvert	Mile Post	Optional
	Diameter	Optional
	Cross Drain Type	Optional
Guardrail	Mile Post	Optional
	Guardrail Side	Optional
	Guardrail Materials	Optional
Sign Complex	Sign Type	Optional
	Sign Materials	Optional
	Sign ID Number	Optional
	Height	Optional
	Width	Optional
	Latitude	Optional
	Longitude	Optional
	Mile Post	Optional
	Map Datum	Not in FAMS
Cattleguard	Mile Post	Optional
	Length	Optional
	Cattleguard Type	Optional
	Width	Optional
Gate	Gate	Optional

Approved National Data Standard for Roads

Asset	Data Element	Status
	Count	Optional
	Mile Post	Optional
	Width	Optional
Culvert	Feature Crossed	Optional
	Federal Highway	Optional
	Fish Passage Provisions	Optional
	Fisheries	Optional
	Hydrologic Unit Code	Optional
	Inspection Damage	Optional
	Inspection Inventory	Optional
	Inspection Routine	Optional
	IR3	Optional
	IR32	Optional
	IR33	Optional
	IRDA	Optional
	IRSA	Optional
	Jurisdiction	Optional
	Maintenance Level	Optional
	Maintenance Responsibility	Optional
	Mile Post	Optional
	ORALL	Optional
	Pipe Number	Optional
	PL33	Optional
	PL32	Optional
	Major Culvert	Optional
	PL3	Optional
	Storm Comments	Optional
	Storm Duration	Optional
	Storm Frequency	Optional
	Travel Surface	Optional
	Travel Way Width	Optional
	Comment	Optional
	Cover Height—Feet	Optional
	Cover Height—Inches	Optional
	Diameter or Rise—Feet	Optional
	Diameter or Rise—Inches	Optional
	Debris Control Structure	Optional
	End Section Inlet	Optional
	End Section Outlet	Optional

Approved National Data Standard for Roads

Asset	Data Element	Status
	Footing Height—Feet	Optional
	Footing Height—Inches	Optional
	Footing Length—Feet	Optional
	Footing Length—Inches	Optional
	Footing Width—Feet	Optional
	Footing Width—Inches	Optional
	Gauge	Optional
	Gauge Code	Optional
	Headwall In	Optional
	Headwall Out	Optional
	Length—Feet	Optional
	Length—Inches	Optional
	Material Shape	Optional
	Rise of Pipe	Optional
	Shape	Optional
	Special	Optional
	Span—Feet	Optional
	Span—Inches	Optional
	Waterway	Optional

Proposed National Data Standard for Primitive Roads

Asset	Data Element	Status
Road	Latitude	Required
	Longitude	Required
	Meridian	Required
	Township	Required
	Range	Required
	Section	Required
	Aliquot Part	Required
	Functional Class	Required
	Seismic Zone	Optional
	Congressional District	Required
	Locator Code	Required
	Easements Needed	Required
	Admin State	Required
	Geographic State	Required
	OR–CA Land	Required
	Route Number	Required
	Spur Number	Required
	Begin Route	Required
	Terminus	Required
	Year Withdrawn	Required
	Road Restrictions	Optional
	County	New in Phase II
	Jurisdiction	New in Phase II
	Master AUC	New in Phase II
Segment	Begin Mile	Required
	End Mile	Required
	Open in Jan	Optional
	Open in Feb	Optional
	Open in Mar	Optional
	Open in Apr	Optional
	Open in May	Optional
	Open in Jun	Optional
	Open in Jul	Optional
	Open in Aug	Optional
	Open in Sep	Optional
	Open in Oct	Optional
	Open in Nov	Optional
	Open in Dec	Optional

Proposed National Data Standard for Primitive Roads

Asset	Data Element	Status
	County	Required
	Jurisdiction	Required
	Maintenance Responsibility	Required
	Maintenance Intensity	Required
	Condition (On Main Screen)	Required
	Surface Type	Required
	Average Width	Required
	Restrictions	Optional
	Asset Category Code (On Main Screen)	Required
	Year Constructed	Optional
	Design Speed	Optional
	OR–CA Land	Required
	Year Withdrawn	Optional
	Road Restrictions	Optional
	Road Surface	Required
	Congressional District	Required
	Meridian	Required
	Township	Required
	Range	Required
	Section	Required
	Aliquot Part	Required
Drain Dip	Mile Post	Optional
	Square Feet	Optional
	Depth	Optional
Water Bar	Mile Post	Optional
	Square Feet	Optional
	Height	Optional
	Water Bar (Deleted)	Optional
Leadoff Ditch	Mile Post	Optional
	Location	Optional
	Leadoff Ditch (Deleted)	Optional
	Length	Optional
Low Water Crossing	Mile Post	Optional

Proposed National Data Standard for Primitive Roads

Asset	Data Element	Status
	Square Feet	Optional
	Low Water Crossing Material	Optional
	Low Water Crossing (Deleted)	Optional
Ford	Mile Post	Optional
	Ford (Deleted)	Optional
Check Dam	Mile Post	Optional
	Check Dam (Deleted)	Optional
	Location	Optional
Rock Spillway	Mile Post	Optional
	Rock Spillway	Optional
Cross Drain Culvert	Mile Post	Optional
	Diameter	Optional
	Cross Drain Type	Optional
Guardrail	Mile Post	Optional
	Guardrail Side	Optional
	Guardrail Materials	Optional
Sign Complex	Sign Type	Optional
	Sign Materials	Optional
	Sign ID Number	Optional
	Height	Optional
	Width	Optional
	Latitude	Optional
	Longitude	Optional
	Mile Post	Optional
Cattleguard	Mile Post	Optional
	Length	Optional
	Cattleguard Type	Optional
	Width	Optional
Gate	Gate	Optional
	Count	Optional
	Mile Post	Optional

Proposed National Data Standard for Primitive Roads

Asset	Data Element	Status
	Width	Optional
Culvert	Feature Crossed	Optional
	Federal Highway	Optional
	Fish Passage Provisions	Optional
	Fisheries	Optional
	Hydrologic Unit Code	Optional
	Inspection Damage	Optional
	Inspection Inventory	Optional
	Inspection Routine	Optional
	IR3	Optional
	IR32	Optional
	IR33	Optional
	IRDA	Optional
	IRSA	Optional
	Jurisdiction	Optional
	Maintenance Level	Optional
	Maintenance Responsibility	Optional
	Mile Post	Optional
	ORALL	Optional
	Pipe Number	Optional
	PL33	Optional
	PL32	Optional
	Major Culvert	Optional
	PL3	Optional
	Storm Comments	Optional
	Storm Duration	Optional
	Storm Frequency	Optional
	Travel Surface	Optional
	Travel Way Width	Optional
	Comment	Optional
	Cover Height—Feet	Optional
	Cover Height—Inches	Optional
	Diameter or Rise—Feet	Optional
	Diameter or Rise—Inches	Optional
	Debris Control Structure	Optional
	End Section Inlet	Optional
	End Section Outlet	Optional

Proposed National Data Standard for Primitive Roads

Asset	Data Element	Status
	Footing Height—Feet	Optional
	Footing Height—Inches	Optional
	Footing Length—Feet	Optional
	Footing Length—Inches	Optional
	Footing Width—Feet	Optional
	Footing Width—Inches	Optional
	Gauge	Optional
	Gauge Code	Optional
	Headwall In	Optional
	Headwall Out	Optional
	Length—Feet	Optional
	Length—Inches	Optional
	Material Shape	Optional
	Rise of Pipe	Optional
	Shape	Optional
	Special	Optional
	Span—Feet	Optional
	Span—Inches	Optional
	Waterway	Optional

Proposed National Data Standard for Trails

Asset	Data Element	Status
Trail	Latitude	Required
	Longitude	Required
	Meridian	Required
	Township	Required
	Range	Required
	Section	Required
	Aliquot Part	Required
	Functional Class	Required
	Seismic Zone	Optional
	Congressional District	Required
	Locator Code	Required
	Easements Needed	Required
	Admin State	Required
	Geographic State	Required
	OR–CA Land	Required
	Rafting DOD	Optional
	Ski DOD	Optional
	Off Road DOD	Optional
	Route Number	Required
	Spur Number	Required
	Begin Route	Required
	Terminus	Required
	Year Withdrawn	Required
	Trail Restrictions	Optional
	County	Optional
	Jurisdiction	Optional
	Master AUC	Optional
Segment	Begin Mile	Required
	End Mile	Required
	Open in Jan	Optional
	Open in Feb	Optional
	Open in Mar	Optional
	Open in Apr	Optional
	Open in May	Optional
	Open in Jun	Optional
	Open in Jul	Optional
	Open in Aug	Optional

Proposed National Data Standard for Trails

Asset	Data Element	Status
	Open in Sep	Optional
	Open in Oct	Optional
	Open in Nov	Optional
	Open in Dec	Optional
	County	Required
	Jurisdiction	Required
	Maintenance Responsibility	Required
	Maintenance Intensity	Required
	Condition (On Main Screen)	Required
	Surface Type	Required
	Average Width	Required
	Restrictions	Optional
	Asset Category Code (On Main Screen)	Required
	Year Constructed	Optional
	Design Speed	Optional
	Year Withdrawn	Optional
	Trail Restrictions	Optional
	Trail Surface	Required
	Congressional District	Required
	Meridian	Required
	Township	Required
	Range	Required
	Section	Required
	Aliquot Part	Required
Drain Dip	Mile Post	Optional
	Size (Square Feet)	Optional
	Depth	Optional
	Drainage Dip	Optional
Water Bar	Mile Post	Optional
	Size (Square Feet)	Optional
	Height	Optional
Leadoff Ditch	Mile Post	Optional
	Location	Optional
	Size (Square Feet)	

Proposed National Data Standard for Trails

Asset	Data Element	Status
Low Water Crossing	Mile Post	Optional
	Size (Square Feet)	Optional
	Low Water Crossing Material	Optional
Ford	Mile Post	Optional
Check Dam	Mile Post	Optional
	Check Dam	Optional
	Locator Code	Optional
Cross Drain Culvert	Mile Post	Optional
	Diameter	Optional
	Cross Drain Type	Optional
Tunnel	Mile Post	Optional
	Height	Optional
	Width	Optional
	Tunnel Materials	Optional
Guardrail	Mile Post	Optional
	Guardrail Side	Optional
	Guardrail Materials	Optional
Sign Complex	Sign Type	Optional
	Sign Materials	Optional
	Sign ID Number	Optional
	Height	Optional
	Width	Optional
	Latitude	Optional
	Longitude	Optional
	Mile Post	Optional
Cattle Guard	Mile Post	Optional
	Length	Optional
	Cattle Guard Type	Optional
	Width	Optional

Proposed National Data Standard for Trails

Asset	Data Element	Status
Gate	Gate (Material)	Optional
	Count	Optional
	Mile Post	Optional
	Width	Optional
Shoulder	Mile Post Curb	Optional
	Length Curb	Optional
	Mile Post Curb & Gutter	Optional
	Length Curb & Gutter	Optional
	Mile Post Retaining Wall	Optional
	Length Retaining Wall	Optional
	Mile Post Riprap	Optional
	Length Riprap	Optional
	Mile Post Slope Protection	Optional
	Length Slope Protection	Optional
	Mile Post Sidewalk	Optional
	Length Sidewalk	Optional
Structure	Size (Lineal Feet)	Optional
	Structure Type	Optional
Handrail	Handrail Side	Optional
	Handrail Material	Optional
	Size (Lineal Feet)	Optional
Barrier	Mile Post	Optional
	Count	Optional
	Barrier Material	Optional
Loading Ramp	Mile Post	Optional
	Count	Optional
	Material	Optional
Pedestrian Ramp	Mile Post	Optional
	Size (Square Feet)	Optional
	Material	Optional

Attachment 8. Action Plan—National Standard for Transportation Linear Features

Bureau of Land Management

ACTION PLAN	
Subject:	Minimum National Data Standard for Linear Features
Lead:	WO-250
Due Date:	
Reviewer:	
OBJECTIVE 2, RECOMMENDATION 5	

1. **Objective:**

The Objective of this Action Plan is to create a minimum national data standard that will form the "baseline" for the collection of linear feature information across the BLM and allow for aggregation, analysis, and comparison across Field Offices, States, and the BLM.

The BLM does not presently provide guidance or direction on a required minimum data standard for collection during the land-use planning process. As a result, State and Field Office personnel collect a wide range of data during the linear feature inventory process based on an inconsistent set of data standards and naming conventions.

This effort is intended to provide guidance and direction to all BLM personnel and facilitate a common "baseline" of linear feature information across the BLM. It is not intended to preclude BLM personnel from collecting additional information beyond the minimum national standard.

2. **Action Plan Tasks:**
    ♦ Initiate after Approval of the Roads and Trails Terminology Report
    ♦ Assemble Team to develop "draft" minimum national data standard for linear features based on existing standards and efforts.
       • National Trails Data Standard
       • IM 2004-117, Minimum National Data Standard Roads
       • National Integrated Land System (NILS) data standards
       • UTAH BLM GIS Data Standards, January 22, 2004.
       • Recreation Information Management System (RMIS) data requirements
    ♦ Present "draft" minimum national data standards to Recreation Visitor Services Advisory Team (RVSAT) and Engineering Advisory Team (EAT) for concurrence
    ♦ Provide "draft" minimum national data standards to WO-250 and WO-360 for approval
    ♦ Publish minimum national data standards for linear features

3. **Responsible Organization(s):** WO-250 is to provide leadership on the effort and coordinate with WO-360 for consistency and the ability to integrate linear feature data into FAMS in the event linear features become assets.

4. **Outcomes:** Minimum national data standards for all BLM transportation and land-use planning efforts that provide a common baseline while preserving the field's ability to augment the standards to meet location specific requirements.

**Attachment 9. Action Plan—Standard Guidance for Land-Use Planning
Bureau of Land Management**

ACTION PLAN	
Subject:	Standardize BLM Comprehensive Travel Management Planning Guidance in a Single Source Guide to Provide Consistency within BLM
Lead:	WO-250
Due Date:	
Reviewer:	
OBJECTIVE 3, RECOMMENDATION 8	

1.   **Objective:**
     The Objective of this Action Plan is to bring together and standardize existing transportation planning and management guidance in a single location and provide a single approach across the BLM that links to other program initiatives and requirements.

     Travel planning and management guidance is presently contained in several guidance documents and does not provide a consistent policy and approach across the BLM. The ability for successfully implementing comprehensive travel management will enhance the BLM's consistency, allow for improved communication with stakeholders, and provide a more efficient approach to the BLM's planning efforts.

     This effort is intended to provide a common reference and single source of information for all land-use planning efforts.

2.   **Action Plan Tasks:**
     ◆ Initiate after Approval of the Roads and Trails Terminology Report
     ◆ Assemble team to identify existing sources of land-use planning guidance
     ◆ Develop a single standard source guide document for all land-use planning efforts
     ◆ Publish updated land-use planning document for BLM use

3.   **Responsible Organization(s):** The recommended approach is for WO-250 to provide leadership on the effort and coordinate with appropriate BLM programs and Divisions as necessary.

4.   **Outcomes:** The outcome of this effort is a single reference source for all BLM land-use planning that is coordinated with other programs and provides land-use planners with a consistent and efficient reference.

Attachment 10. Action Plan—Removal of Transportation Linear Features

Bureau of Land Management

ACTION PLAN	
Subject:	Develop and Implement a Formalized Approach for Tracking and Removal of Unwanted Linear Features on BLM Land
Lead:	WO-360
Due Date:	
Reviewer:	
OBJECTIVE 3, RECOMMENDATION 10	

1. **Objective:**

   The Objective of this Action Plan is to develop and implement a formal program within BLM that identifies, tracks, and prioritizes unwanted linear features (linear disturbances and existing roads and trails identified for removal) and develops a funding mechanism to support the removal or rehabilitation process without adversely affecting existing limited resources used for annual and deferred maintenance.

   The BLM does not presently have a formal process or program that identifies, tracks, prioritizes, and funds the removal of unwanted linear features. Such a program is essential to the long-term asset management of BLM land and is considered essential by the Roads and Trails Terminology Team.

   This effort is intended to provide a concerted, long-term effort that provides the BLM with a consolidated means of reporting the present levels of unwanted linear features on BLM land and a means for proactively managing their removal and remediation.

2. **Action Plan Tasks:**
   - Initiate after Approval of the Roads and Trails Terminology Report
   - Develop a team composed of key BLM Stakeholders to formulate a recommended program for implementation within the BLM
   - Coordinate the effort with existing land-use planning, asset management, and related activities.
   - Develop a recommended BLM strategy for implementation across the BLM
   - Staff and Manage the effort on an ongoing basis

3. **Responsible Organization(s):** The recommended approach is for WO-360 to provide leadership on the effort with a combined task team that includes engineering and recreation personnel and to coordinate with appropriate BLM programs and Divisions as necessary.

4. **Outcomes:** The outcome of this effort is a strategic, long-term approach for the BLM to use in identifying, tracking, prioritizing, funding, and removing or rehabilitating unwanted linear features on a nationwide basis.

Attachment 11. Trails Data Standards Cross-Walk

TRAILS DATA STANDARDS	
FAMS	**NON-FAMS (e.g., GIS)**
Basic Trail Information	**Basic Trail Information**
Trail Name	Interagency Trail Identifier
Trail Number	Shared System
Length	
Trail Status	
Trail Surface	
Trail Admin Unit & Location	**Trail Admin Unit & Location**
Agency	Municipality
Admin Org	
Managing Agency	
Managing Org	
Congressional District	
County	
Geolocation	
Jurisdiction	
State	
Trail Management and Use	**Trail Management and Use**
Trail Class	Trail System
Primary Trail Maintainer	Road System
	Land Use Plan
	Designed Use
	Managed Use
	Motorized Prohibited
	Prohibited Use
	Accessibility Status
Trail Management Consideration	**Trail Management Consideration**
Rights-of-Way	Historical Significance
	National Trail Designation
	Special Management Area
Trail Condition and Cost	**Trail Condition and Cost**
Trail Condition	Cost: Annual or Cyclic Operations (Rec Sites only)
Cost: Annual or Cyclic Maintenance	Cost: Deferred Maintenance (Imported to FAMS from condition assessments)

TRAILS DATA STANDARDS	
FAMS	**NON-FAMS (e.g., GIS)**
Cost: Last Updated	Cost: Improvement–Construction (Project data sheets, 5-year plans)
Additional NST or NHT Basic Information (Attributes Recorded only to NHTS & NSTS)	**Additional NST or NHT Basic Information (Attributes Recorded only to NHTS & NSTS)**
Visitor Center Name Visitor Facility Location Visitor Facility Type (all three assets listed as facilities—not trails)	NHT/NST Trail Administrator Visitor Facility Activities Visitor Facility Contact Information (all three tracked by RMIS)
NHT Heritage Resource Information (Attributes only to NHT Routes or Associated Heritage Resource Sites)	NHT Heritage Resource Information (Attributes only to NHT Routes or Associated Heritage Resource Sites) Type of Route Type of Site NHT Auto-Tour Surface NHT Certification Status NHT Condition Category NHT High Potential Segment NHT Public Use Segment NHT Potential Segment NHT Public Use Site NHT Site Name NHT Site Number NRHP Criteria NRHP Property Category

7 Oct 2004 Rev 2

Attachment 12. "Name that Linear Feature" Photographs

1.

2.

3.

4.

5.

6.

7.

8.

9.

10.

11.

12.

13.

14.

15.

16.

17.

18.

19.

20.